THE HOLY SPIRIT AND YOU

Emmanuel O. Uthman

THE HOLY SPIRIT AND YOU

Copyright© 2009 By Emmanuel O. Uthman

BIBLE QUOTATIONS FROM NKJV

E-mail: euthman2001@yahoo.com

TABLE OF CONTENTS

CHAPTER ONE

WHO IS THE HOLY SPIRIT

The Holy Spirit is the third person in the Godhead of the Father, Son, and the Holy Spirit. He was at the beginning with God. He was part of creation; He played a significant role in the creation of the world.

"In the beginning, God created the heavens and the earth. The earth was without form, and void, and darkness was on the face of deep, and the Spirit of God was hovering over the face of the waters." Gen.1: 1-2 NKJV.

The first two verses of the Bible spoke about God. The first appearance of God that we saw was the Holy Spirit hovering over the face of the earth. Before God spoke, we saw the Spirit of God moving over the face of the earth. The Holy Spirit was the creative force that created the world.

The Holy Spirit is God, He was not created, He was with God from the beginning. The Holy Spirit had all the attributes of God.

> i. The Holy Spirit is **Omnipotent**.
> ii. The Holy Spirit is **Omniscience**.
> iii. The Holy Spirit is **Omnipresence**

These attributes make God different from man and all His creations including Satan. No creation possessed any of these three attributes.

The Holy Spirit is all-powerful, there is nothing that He cannot do, capable of all things because is Omnipotent. The Holy Spirit is not power but He produces power. He also empowered the people of God to do more than what a superpower can do.

"So he answered and said to me: This is the word of the Lord to Zerubbabel: Not by might nor by power, but by My Spirit says the Lord of hosts "Zech. 4: 6 NKJV

The Holy Spirit will empower the believer with the Almighty power of God, to do great and mainly things. Jesus promised the Holy Spirit to the church as an equipper and empowering Spirit of God.

"Behold, I send the promise of my Father upon you; but tarry in the city of Jerusalem until you are endued with power from on high."Luke.24: 49 NKJV.

"But you shall receive power when the Holy Spirit has come upon you, and you shall be witnesses to Me in Jerusalem, and in all Judea, and Samaria, and to the end of the earth." Acts 1: 8 NKJV.

The Holy Spirit empowered Samson to do the impossible; he carried the gates of a city. That incredible demonstration of God's power. The Holy Spirit empowered Mary a virgin to give birth to a baby without a relationship with a man

 "And the angel answered and said to her, the Holy Spirit will come upon you, and the power of the Highest will overshadow you; therefore, also that Holy One who is to be born will be called the Son of God. For with God nothing will be impossible." Lk.1: 35, 37. NKJV

The Holy Spirit is the power of God that brings God's plans into actualization. Our Lord was empowered by the Holy Spirit.

"How God anointed Jesus of Nazareth with the Holy Spirit and power, and how he went around ding good and healing all who were under the power of the devil, because God was with him."

Acts 20: 38 NIV

Through the enablement of the Holy Spirit, great things can be done. There is nothing God cannot do; the Holy Spirit is the agent of God that is doing it. Any power outside the enablement of the Holy Spirit is not of God. The power of God can be real in our lives as we walk in the Holy Spirit. The Acts of Apostles are the Acts of the Holy Spirit; it was the Holy Spirit that gave power to the Apostles. They were timid, fearful, and confused after the crucifixion of the Lord Jesus Christ. The presence of the Holy Spirit in their lives brought confidence into their lives. Every believer needs the Holy Spirit, "Ye shall receive power after the Holy Spirit comes upon you." When the Holy Spirit comes into your life, you will have the power to do exploit.

The Holy Spirit is God:

"God is Spirits, and those that worship Him must worship in Spirit and truth."

Jn.4: 24 NKJV

God said to Abraham:

> *"When Abraham was ninety-nine years old, the LORD appeared to Abram and said to him, "I am Almighty God walk before Me and be blameless." Gen.17: 1 NKJV*

In the Old Testament God related with men, giving us his name as Jehovah, depending on the circumstance, Jehovah is able to do all things. Jehovah promised to send us a Saviour. Jesus Christ the Son of God, came to save us from our sin. His name was Immanuel meaning God with us. He was born through a woman, left behind his glory as God, lived as a man among us, ate with us, hated by us and the creator was crucified by His creatures.

> *"And without controversy great is the mystery of godliness: God was manifested in the flesh, justified in the Spirit, seen by angels, preached among the Gentiles, believed on in the world, received up in glory."*

"In the beginning was the word, and the word was with God, and the Word was God. He was at the beginning with God..."

And the word became flesh and dwelt among us and we beheld His glory, the glory as of the only begotten of the Father, full of grace and truth."

Jn.1: 1-2, 14 NKJV

God in the Old Testament promised us the outpouring of His Spirit upon all flesh.

"And it shall come to pass afterward That I will pour out my Spirit on all flesh; your sons and your daughters shall prophesy, your old men shall see visions. And also on my men servants and on My maidservants will pour out my Spirit in those days."

Joel 2: 28-29.

The Holy Spirit we are receiving today is the spirit of God. The Spirit of God is not inferior to God. When Jesus Christ was about to leave the planet earth He promised to send the Holy Spirit. The Holy Spirit is representing the Lord Jesus Christ on earth. He is standing for Christ. The way Jesus related to His disciples, is the way the Holy Spirit is to relate with individual members of the body of Christ. The Holy Spirit is the representative of Godhead on earth, in the believer's life, in the church, and in the world today.

"But now I go away to Him who sent Me, and none of you asks Me, "Where are you going?" But because I have said these things to you, sorrow has filled your heart. Nevertheless, I tell you the truth. It is to your advantage that I go away; for if I do not go away, the Helper will not come, He will convict the world of sin, and of righteousness because I go to My Father and you see Me no more; of judgment, because the ruler of this world is judged ... However, when He, the Spirit of truth, has come, He will

guide you into all truth; for He will not speak on His own authority, but whatever He hears He will speak; He will tell you things to come. He will glorify Me, for He will take of what is Mine and declare it to you. All things that the Father has are Mine. Therefore, I said that He will take of Mine and declare it to you."

Jn.16: 5-10; 12-15.

The Holy Spirit was promised by the Father, to be our comforter, guide, counselor, teacher, advocate, stand-by, and strengthener. Just like Jesus Christ was sent by God to be our Saviour. The Holy Spirit is here to prepare us for Heaven: he was the promised of the Father.

"And being assembled together with them, he commanded them not to depart from Jerusalem, but to wait for the Promise of the Father, "Which," He said, "You have heard from Me; for John truly baptized with water, but you shall be baptized with the Holy Spirit not many days from now." Acts 1: 4-5 NKJV

The Holy Spirit is the promised of the Father to the church of Christ. We need the Holy Spirit in our lives.

He will power us to do great and mighty things for God. He will enable us to ring many Sons and Daughters to God. The Holy Spirit preserves the church from the pollution of the world. He guides the church into all truth. We must welcome the Holy Spirit into our lives. We must be full of the Holy Spirit; every Christian must seek the fullness of the Holy Spirit. We need Him to make progress in life and ministry. We must walk in the Spirit. Receive the Holy Spirit in Jesus' name.

"Father, I pray for the persons reading this book that the eyes of their understanding be opened, that they may know Him, whom you have sent to be our comforter, that they may relax with Him as God, honor Him, pray to Him and walk

with Him in every area of their lives. In Jesus name, I pray (Amen)."

CHAPTER TWO

THE PERSON OF THE HOLY SPIRIT

The Holy Spirit is a person, we should relate with Him as a person not just a power, a tongue, a force, or a gift that we can take and use, as we want. God is a being at the creation of man, God said:

> *"Then God said. "Let Us make man in Our image, according to Our likeness; let them have dominion over the fish of the sea, over the birds of the air and over the cattle, over all the earth and over every creeping thing creeps on the earth." So God created man in His own image; in the image of God He created him; male and female He created them."*
>
> *Gen.1: 26-27 NKJV*

We are created in the image of God, we are in His likeness. The Holy Spirit is God, He's not to be treated as a thing. He must be treated with honor and respect as the Creator of Heaven and Earth. He is worthy of worship and fellowship.

> *"The grace of the Lord Jesus Christ, and the Love of God, and the communion of the Holy Spirit be with you all (Amen)."*
>
> *2 Cor.13: 14.*

We all share the benediction and speak of the sweet communion of the Holy Spirit. The word communion signifies fellowship, two fellows in a ship, having an agreement, you cannot fellowship with an intimate thing you cannot fellowship with an object, there are many symbols of the Holy Spirit, like fire, dove, etc. good as they communicate to us about is a person. The fact still remain that the Holy Spirit is a person with all the manifested attributes of His personality.

If we are going to succeed in life and ministry, we must know the Holy Spirit and relate with Him as a person, every Christian worker, minister must be sensitive to the Holy Spirit.

Our ability to perform depends largely on our relationship with the Holy Spirit. Kathin Kulmen called the Holy Spirit my closeth friend; she will not want to do anything to grieve the Holy Spirit in her service. She was mightily used in the healing and miracle ministry, she was not just having the gifts of healing, but befriend to the giver of the healing gifts.

David Youngi Cho, the Pastor of the world's largest single congregation church, said the Holy Spirit is my senior partner, he related with the Holy Spirit, speak with the Holy Spirit, and pray in the Spirit.

Paul the Apostle walked in the Spirit, the Holy Spirit in his missionary activities, he wanted to go some places but the Holy Spirit forbid him, he know how to walk with the Holy Spirit, but he did not receive the Holy Spirit as a gift to be used, but as a person to enable him to succeed in the ministry.

> *"Now when they had gone through Phrygia and the region of Galatia, they were forbidden by the Holy Spirit to preach the word in Asia. After they had come to Mysia, they tried to go into Bithynia, but the Spirit did not permit them."*
>
> *Acts 16: 6-7.*

Peter had an encounter with the Holy Spirit as he was sent to minister to the house of Cornelius, he was reluctant but the Spirit mandated him to go.

> *"When Peter thought about the vision, the Spirit said to him, "Behold, three men are seeking you. Arise therefore, go down and go with them, doubting nothing; for I have sent them."*

> *Acts 10: 19-20 NKJV*

Philip was having a successful evangelistic outreach at Samaria but the Holy Spirit gave him another call to minister to the man of Ethiopia.

> *"Then the Spirit said to Philip, "Go near and overtake this chariot."*

> *Acts 8: 29 NKJV*

If the Holy Spirit is not a person He cannot relate with them in such a personal way.

I want us to further look at the evidence of His human attributes:

    I.   The Holy Spirit speaks:

"However, when He, the spirit of truth, has come, He will guide you into all truth; for He will on His own authority, but whatever He hears He will speak; glorify Me, for He will speak on His own and He will show you things to come. He will glorify Me, for He will take of what is Mine and declare it to you. All things that the Father has are

Mine. Therefore I said that He will take of Mine and declare it to you."

> *John 16: 13-15 NKJV*

Jesus said, the Holy Spirit will speak to us, He reveal the plans of God to us, and the Holy Spirit is still speaking today.

> *"Now the Spirit expressly says that in latter times some will depart from the faith giving heed to deceiving spirits and*

doctrines of demons.

1 Tim.4: 1 NKJV

Our God is not dumb, the Holy Spirit is God and He can speak and communicate to God's people the will of God.

II.   The Spirit could be silent.

"Do not quench the spirit."

1 Thess.5: 19 NKJV

You can silence the Holy Spirit in your life. He will not force you, because His a gentle Spirit. Samson went on doing his own thing and did not know when the Holy Spirit left him.

When you persist in doing your own thing, the Holy Spirit will keep quiet.

> **"And the Lord said, "My Spirit shall not strive with man forever, for he is indeed flesh; yet his days shall be one hundred and twenty years."**

Gen.6: 3 NKJV

You must learn to yield to the prompting of the Holy Spirit. The devil will force you, pressurized you, intimidate and harass you to do their bidding, but the Holy Spirit is . Surrender your life to Him. Let Him have His way in you. He will never hurt you, He will do you good all the days of your life. He loves you, listen to the Holy Spirit, He will speak to you, through the pages of your Bible, He can speak to you as you are on your knees in prayer, He can speak to you while you are seated in church, He can speak to you as lay down on your bed. Let me share this personal experience with you. Some years ago, I read Rev.3: 1-6, I was meditating on verse 2, 1 was on my three-setter chair, I laid down and fell asleep, in my sleep, I found myself in a community, I was in a house of an old man, full grey hair, I told the old man, I wanted to rest my body, so I slept on a three-seater chair in the old man's house. There had a dream, giving me instructions about my ministry. I woke up in the old man's house and the old man called me and the old man called me and gave me instructions, and an understanding of certain development in my ministry. I thanked the old man and went away and suddenly found myself in my seating room on my three-setters with my Bible by my side.

I knew the Lord had spoken to me, concerning His plans for my life and ministry.

Listen to the Holy Spirit; let Him reveal the plans of God for your life. He will show you the way that you must go.

> *"He who has an ear, let him hear what the Spirit says to the churches."*
>
> *Rev.3: 13.*

Will you listen to Him or silence him? Remember He loves you.

III.   The Holy Spirit Can Be Grieved or Hurt as a Person.

"But they rebelled and grieved His Holy Spirit. So He Himself against them as an enemy, and He fought against them."

> *Isa.63: 10 NKJV*

"And do not grieve the Holy Spirit of God, by whom you were sealed for the day of redemption."

> *Eph.4: 30 NKJV*

You cannot grieve a thing or an object, but you grieve a person, even you can grieve the Holy Spirit because of His a person.

The children of Israel in the wilderness need the Spirit of God. My prayer is that you will not grieve the Holy Spirit.

IV.   **The Holy Spirit Can Be Sinned Against.**

Jesus warned against sin, against the Holy Spirit. Only those who have known the Lord and had been partakers of the divine experience can sin against the Holy Spirit. The Jews knew the Holy Spirit; they spoke against Him deliberately, because they don't want to believe in the ministry of the Lord Jesus Christ as the Son of God. They gave the glory meant for God to the devil. They by that act blasphemed the Holy Spirit.

> *"He who is not with Me is against Me, and he who does not gather with Me scatters abroad. Therefore I say to you, every sin and blasphemy will be forgiven men, but the blasphemy against the Spirit will not be forgiven men. Anyone who speaks a word against the Son of man, it will be forgiven him; but whoever speaks against the Holy Spirit, it will not be forgiven him, either in this age or in the age to come."*

> *Matt. 12: 31-32 NKJV*

Because the Holy Spirit is a person we can sin against Him. In the Early Church, a couple died for lying to the Holy Spirit.

> *"But Peter said, "Ananias, why has Satan filled your heart to lie to the Holy Spirit and keep back part of the price of the land for yourself?*

> *… You have not lied to men but to God … Then Peter said to her, "How is it that you have agreed together to test the Spirit of the Lord?"*

> *Acts 5: 3, 4, 9 NKJV*

The Holy Spirit is God; his all-knowing nothing can be hidden from Him. He knows all things, he sees all things. You cannot lie to the Spirit of the Lord. Acknowledge your sin, confess them, repent of them and ask for cleansing in the blood of Jesus. The Holy Spirit convinces us of sins and wrongdoing in our lives, when He does, humble yourself and for the sake of your sinful ways.

> *"Can anyone hide himself in secret places, so I shall not see him? Says the LORD. Do I not fill heaven and earth?" Says the LORD."*
>
> *Jer.23: 24 NKJV*

The Spirit of God is everywhere; every secret sin are open before Him. Get out of your sinful habits; the Spirit of God is seeing you.

Start a new relationship with the Holy Spirit, your Marker, your Guide, your Counsellor, your Comforter, your Teacher, your Advocate, and your friend. Thank you Holy Spirit.

> *"Holy Spirit I ask that you will reveal yourself to this my brother or thus my sister, that we may know you, walk with you and be refreshed by you in the walk with Christ Jesus."*

The Holy Spirit is a Minister and Executive agent of God on earth.

CHAPTER THREE

THE MINISTRIES OF THE HOLY SPIRIT TO BELIEVERS

"But the Helper, the Holy Spirit, whom the Father will send in My name, He will teach you all things, bring to your remembrance all things that I said to you." Jn.16: 26 NKJV

The Holy Spirit is our Helper. He came as a ministering Spirit to minister to the saints, the church, and to the world.

Jesus came to save us and deliver us from our enemy. The Holy Spirit is here to HELP us to make the will of God possible.

Ministry is a service. The Holy Spirit is a Minister and Executive agent of God on earth. He's in charge of God's business on earth today. I want us to look at His threefold ministry:

    i.   His Ministry to the Believers

    ii.   His Ministry to the Church

    iii. His Ministry to the World.

TO BELIEVERS: The Holy Spirit has five-fold ministry to the individual believers in Christ.

"But the Helper, the Holy Spirit whom the Father will send in My name, He will teach you all things, and bring to remembrance all things that I said to you."   *Jn.15: 26 NKJV*

OUR COUNSELLOR: The Holy Spirit gives counsel so that we shall not be confused. You must draw from the wisdom of the Holy Spirit.

> *"The Spirit of the Lord rest upon Him, The Spirit of wisdom and understanding, the Spirit of counsel and might, the Spirit of knowledge and of the fear of the Lord." Isa.11: 2 NKJV*

You need counsel every area of your life, the Holy Spirit will be available to give you counsel in any area of your life. He will advise about what you should do, to fulfill the will of God for your life.

> *"Counsel is mine, sound wisdom; I am understanding, I have strength."   Pro.8: 14 NKJV*

The Holy Spirit is the agent of God that releases God's wisdom into our lives.

> *"But God has revealed them to us through His spirit. For the Spirit searches all things, yes, the deep things of God. For what man knows the things of a man except for the Spirit of the man which is in him? Even so no one knows the things of God except the Spirit of God. Now we have received, not the Spirit of the world, but the Spirit who is from God, that might know the things that have been freely given to us by God."   1 Cor.2: 10-12 NKJV*

We have the privilege to enjoy divine wisdom, as we draw from the Holy Spirit.

OUR HELPER: When God created Adam, He saw the need to create and Helper from him. God created a woman to be a helper to the man.

> *"And the Lord God said, "It is not good that man should be alone; I will make him a helper comparable to him." Gen.2: 18 NKJV*

God said, "I will make him a helper comparable to him." When

God thought of a helper for man, He thought of a being comparable to man, somebody of almost equal status with him. Somebody he could draw strength from, at the time of crisis somebody to stand as assistance to him. Somebody to support him in his weakness.

The Holy Spirit is our helper, He will stand by our side, and share our burden as no one can do.

He will help us and deliver us from our enemies. God knows we have to face the battles of life, the Holy Spirit is there to provide help and deliverance for us.

> *"But I am poor and needy; make haste to me, O God! You are my help and my deliverer, O Lord, do not delay." Ps.70: 5 NKJV*

Don't be intimated by life challenges, the Holy Spirit will help you. God promised to help you, the agent of God that provides you instant help is the Holy Spirit, at the moment of emergence, He will be there for you.

> *"Fear not, for I am with you; be not dismayed, for I am your God. I will strengthen you, yes,*
>
> *I will help you, I will uphold you with my righteous right hand."   Isa.41: 10 NKJV*

Fear is of the devil, have faith in God. Trust in God, the Holy Spirit is here to give you that assurance that God will help you. Draw from the strength of the Holy Spirit inside of you. God will help you.

OUR ADVOCATE: This legal term for a lawyer who presents a client case in a law court, the devil is our accuser.

> *"Then I heard a loud voice saying in heaven, "Now salvation, and strength, and the kingdom of our God, and the power of His Christ have come, for the accuser of our brethren, who*

> *accused them before our God day and night, has been cast down." Rev.12: 10 NKJV*

We have an enemy, a thief a destroyer called the Devil, seeking whom he will devour:

> *"Be sober, be vigilant because your adversary the devil walks about like a roaring lion, seeking whom he may devour." 1 Pet.5: 8 NKJV*

The Holy Spirit is our advocate against the Devil. An advocate is one called alongside to help when the devil comes with his accusation the Holy Spirit will raise a defense for us.

Praise the Lord!

> *"… When the enemy comes in like a flood, the Spirit of the Lord will lift up a standard against him." Isa.59: 19[b]*

You have an advocate with the Father, a team of legal backup to defend you against the flood of accusations and intimidating evidence that your enemy had – Jesus and the Holy Spirit will stand for your defense – Praise the Lord!

> *"My little children, these things I write to you, so that you may not sin. And if anyone sins, we have an advocate with the Father, Jesus Christ the righteous. And He Himself is the propitiation for our sins, and not for ours only but also for the whole world." 1 Jn.2: 1-2 NKJV*

God will defend you against your enemy, the agent of God that will advocate your case in the court of life problems and oppositions is the Holy Spirit.

OUR INTERCESSOR: The Holy Spirit intercedes for us, He acts by speaking on our behalf, procuring favor for us, to persuade God to have pity on us and deliver us from our difficulties. He prays the mind of God for us.

> *"Likewise the Spirit also helps in our weaknesses. For we do*

not know what we should pray for as we ought, but the Spirit Himself makes intercession for us with groaning which cannot be uttered. Now He who searches the hearts knows what the mind of the Spirit is, because He makes intercession for the saints according to the will of God."

Rom.8: 26-27.

The Holy Spirit stands in the gap between us and God, pleading our cause before God. He prays through us, when you pray in the Spirit by using your prayer language, the Holy Spirit will help you pray for a situation you don't know what is going on or about to happen.

Jesus Christ is praying for us in Heaven, the Holy Spirit will link up prayer alert from within us to call for prayer. We like an airplane that as it communication gadget connected to the tower. The Holy Spirit is inside of the believer, praying for you, spotting danger, He will alert our savior and High Priest on areas of our weaknesses. He knows the soft spot in your life.

"For we do not have a High Priest who cannot sympathize with our weaknesses, but was in all points tempted as we are, yet without sin. let us, therefore, come boldly to the throne of grace, that we may obtain mercy and find grace to help in time of need."Heb.4: 15-16 NKJV

Every one of us needs people who are praying for us if you are not sure of anybody praying for you. I want to assure you, that the Holy Spirit is praying for you. The Holy Spirit will also move other people to pray for you. You have a prayer partner in the Holy Spirit; let Him pray through you, for you and your loved ones.

OUR STRENGTHENER: The Holy Spirit gives us continuous strength to go on with life. Give us tremendous strength to face life battles. Strength in weakness.

"Have you not known? Have you not heard? The everlasting

> *God, the Lord, The Creator of the ends of the earth, neither faints nor weary. His understanding is unsearchable. He gives power to the weak, and to those who have no might He gives power to the weak, and to those who have no might He increases strength. Even the youths shall faint and be weary, and the young men shall utterly fall, but those who wait on the Lord shall renew their strength; they shall mount up with wings like eagles, they shall run and not be weary, they shall walk and not faint."* **Phil.4: 13 NKJ**

The Holy Spirit is the agent of God, which gives us continuous courage to continue in the Christian journey. Onward Christian soldier, marching on to life.

I remember my days in the primary school, our school and other school were running 400 meters race, our school representative was the youngest, he started running well ahead of others, but his strength was failing, those of us who were spectators supporting kept shouting his name, to keep running, he kept on running on the strength of our shout and made it to the end. Keep on going in the strength of the Holy Spirit.

> *"It is God who arms me with strength, and makes my way perfect." Ps.18: 32 NKJV*

THE MINISTRIES OF THE HOLY SPIRIT TO THE CHURCH AND THE WORLD

Because this book is concerned with the Holy Spirit and the individual of Christ – that is you and me. I will not write much about His ministry to the church and the world, but I will write briefly in summary:

His ministries to the church which is the body of Christ in the world.

    i.   Guide the church into all truth.

    ii.   Reveal the will of the Father to the church.

iii.   Guide the church into the future.

iv.   The Holy Spirit will ensure that Christ Jesus is honored.

v.   The Holy Spirit will build the church of Christ.

The scripture for this truth is Jn.16: 13-14. I quote:

> *"However, when He, the Spirit of truth, has come, He will guide you into all truth; for He will not speak; and He will tell you things to come. He will glorify Me, for He will take of what is Mine and declare it to you."*

The Holy Spirit is the One preserving the church from error. Any church where the Holy Spirit is not active, that church will be in darkness.

His ministries to the world.

> *"And when He comes, He will convict the world of sin, and of righteousness because I go to my*
>
> *Father and you see Me no more; of judgment, because the ruler of this world is judged."*

> *Jn.16: 8-11 NKJV*

These are the fold ministries to the world.

i.   He will convince the world of sin. The Holy Spirit convinces the sinners of his sin.

ii.   He will demonstrate signs and wonders, to confirm the message of the gospel as a witness of God.

iii.   He will preserve the truth of the Gospel, and act as salt to preserve the message of salvation.

iv.   He will bring judgment upon the world and

those who wants to hinder the Gospel.

v.   He will lead the sinners to accept Christ as their personal Saviour.

We need the Holy Spirit to succeed in life and ministry.

CHAPTER FOUR

BAPTISM IN THE HOLY SPIRIT

There are two stages of the Holy Spirit in the believer's life, when we gave our lives to Christ, we receive a measure of the Holy Spirit.

> *"And will put my Spirit within you and caused you to walk in my statutes, and ye shall keep my judgments, and do them."*

> *Ezek.36: 27*

When Jesus came into your heart, the Holy Spirit becomes residence in your hear. Dwelling in your heart.

> *"Even the Spirit of truth; whom the world cannot receive, because it seeth him not, neither knoweth him; but ye know him; for he dwelleth with you and shall be in you."*

> *Jn.14: 17*

The Holy Spirit dwells in you. If you are a child of God, you already had the indwelling presence of the Holy Spirit in you. But you still need to be baptized in the Holy Spirit. Jesus said – "Which is in you and shall be in you" there are two points of the entrance of the Holy Spirit into the believer's life. The first instance is at salvation to bear witness with you that you are now a child of God.

> *"The Spirit Himself bears witness with our spirit that we are children of God."*

Romans 8: 16 NKJV

The presence of the Holy Spirit at this stage in our life is to confirm the presence of Jesus Christ in our life. When you ask Jesus into your life, He comes in the Spirit, you don't see physical Jesus in your heart, the Spirit of Jesus, come and indwell in you, the Spirit of Jesus is the Spirit of God and the Spirit of God is the Holy Spirit.

> *"But you are not in the flesh but in the Spirit, if indeed the Spirit of God dwells in you. Now if anyone does not have the Spirit of Christ, he is not His." Romans 8: 9 NKJV*

You are a child of God because you received Jesus Christ into your life, the Spirit of God is in you. You still need to be baptized in the Holy Spirit. The word baptism is taken from the Greek word "Baptzo" which means to "Immerse" or "Buried." When you are baptized in the Holy Spirit you are immersed in the Holy Spirit. Let me illustrate it. Take a clean glass cup, and put water into it, that cup will contain water. Take a bowl of water submerge the cup into it, will have water in and out around it. When you are baptized in the Holy Spirit, you just don't have the Holy Spirit; you are clothed in the Holy Spirit.

> *"Behold, I send the Promise of My Father upon you, but tarry in the city of Jerusalem until you are endued with, power from on high."*

> *Lk.24: 49 NKJV*

To be "Endued" is to be clothed with or be worn by. The Holy Spirit will empower you, for service. The second entrance of the Holy Spirit into our life is to empower us to be witnesses of Jesus. To give us the ability to do the work of God. *"But you shall receive power when the Holy Spirit has come upon you; and you shall be witnesses to Me." Acts 1: 8*

We need the Holy Spirit to do the work of God, the arm of flesh cannot prevail, and without the baptism of the Holy Spirit, we cannot demonstrate the power of God. Any power demonstrated without the Holy Spirit is not of God. You must desire the baptism of the Holy Spirit to be a witness of Jesus.

> *"And the witness of Jesus the whole multitude. And they chose Stephen, a man full of faith and the Holy Spirit ... and Stephen, full of faith and power, did great wonders and signs among the people."*   *Acts 6: 5, 8 NKJV*

Nobody is qualify to be a Christian worker who is not baptized in the Holy Spirit, every believer must seek the experience of the baptism in the Holy Spirit.

Jesus Christ our Saviour is our Baptizer in the Holy Spirit. He will baptize you after you had received Him. Your Pastor baptized you in water. The Holy Spirit baptized you into the body of Christ.

> *"I indeed baptize you with water unto repentance, but He who is coming after me is*
>
> *mightier than I, whose sandals I am not worthy to carry. He will baptize you with the Holy Spirit and fire."*   *Matt.3: 11 NKJV*

How to Be Baptized In the Holy Spirit.

You must thirst for the Holy Spirit; there must be a desire for Him before you can be baptized. Do you desire the Holy Spirit, if your answer is yes, you can have the Holy Spirit, and the power of God can come into your life right now?

> *"On the last day, that great day of the feast, Jesus stood and cried out saying, "if anyone thirsts, let him come to Me and drink. He who believes in Me, as the scripture has said, out of his heart will flow rivers of living water. But this He spoke concerning the Spirit, whom those believing in Him would*

> *receive; for the Holy Spirit was not yet given because Jesus was not yet glorified."*

> *Jn.7:37-39 NKJV*

The Holy Spirit is God; you must desire Him, in your life. If you are born-again, the Holy Spirit is already inside of you. If you are not born-again, you cannot receive the Holy Spirit. You must first receive Jesus Christ as your personal Lord and Saviour before you can receive the Holy Spirit.

> *"Then Peter said to them "Repent, and let every one of you be baptized in the name of Jesus Christ for the remission of sins, and you shall receive the gift of the Holy Spirit. For the promise is to you and to your children, and to all who are afar off, as many as the Lord our God will call."*

> *Acts 2: 38: 39 NKJV*

The Holy Spirit is a promise to those who believed in the Lord Jesus Christ. You must love God, you must love Jesus, love the Holy Spirit.

> *"Therefore, he who rejects this does not reject man, but God, who has also given us His Holy Spirit."*   *Eph.4: 8 NKJV*

The Holy Spirit is a gift, you must receive Him by faith, and you don't need to cry, beg and weep to receive Him. Ask in faith to say, "Father, I come to you in Jesus name to receive the gift of the Holy Spirit." Believe that God will give you, you don't have to struggle or make it up, simply ask in faith in Jesus name and you will be given.

> *"This only want to learn from you: Did you receive the Spirit by the works of the law, or by the hearing of faith ... therefore, He who suppliers the Spirit to you and works miracles among you, does He do it by the works of the law, or by the hearing of faith?"*

Gal.3: 2, 5 NKJV

The Holy Spirit is a gift; we receive Him by asking the Father in Jesus' name. When you ask, you shall be given; God will never deny you the answer to your request for the Holy Spirit.

> *"If you then, being evil, know how to give good gifts to your children, how much more will your heavenly Father give the Holy Spirit to those who ask Him."* *Lk.11: 13 NKJV*

FIVE STEPS TO RECEIVING THE HOLY SPIRIT

STEP ONE: Acknowledge Christ in your life, and confess Him as your personal Lord and Saviour. Ask for cleansing in the blood of every known sin in your life.

STEP TWO: Ask in faith, ask the Father to give you the Holy Spirit. Ask in the name of Jesus. Jesus is the Baptizer in the Holy Spirit. Believe that God will give you the Holy Spirit, and thank Him for giving you, the Holy Spirit.

STEP THREE: Keep quiet after you had asked in faith and given thanks. Remain quiet don't speak in any language you have learned before, remain quiet. The Holy Spirit will give you utterance, the ability to speak and pray in the language you hand never learned before.

> *"And they were all filled with Holy Spirit and began to speak with other tongues as the Spirit gave them utterance.'*

> *Acts 2: 4 NKJV*

The Holy Spirit will not speak through you, but He will you utterance to speak in a new tongue.

STEP FOUR: Open your mouth and begin to speak in a new, unlearned language as you receive the enablement from Holy

Spirit. You will do, the speaking as the Holy Spirit gives you the utterance. You can speak in a new tongue.

The evidence that you have received the Holy Spirit is your ability to pray in other tongues. It is very exciting and refreshing when you pray in your tongue. It may be like stammering, it may not make sense, just continue as you grow in the Spirit, and you will be experiencing growth in your ability to pray in other tongues.

> *"For with stammering lips and another tongue. He will speak to these people."Isa.28: 11 NKJV*

STEP FIVE: Sing in a new tongue, singing in the Spirit will develop your ability to pray in the Holy Spirit.

> *"What is the conclusion then? I will pray with the Spirit, and I will also pray with understanding. I will sing with the understanding."   1 Cor.14: 15 NKJV*

You can use these steps to lead others to the baptism of the Holy Spirit. Receive the Holy Spirit.

www.ingramcontent.com/pod-product-compliance
Lightning Source LLC
Chambersburg PA
CBHW050624160726
48003CB00003B/1324